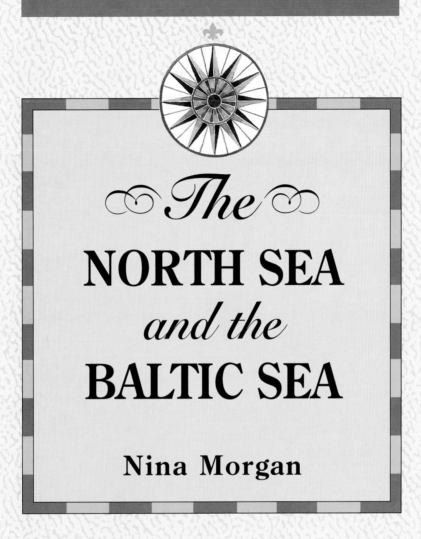

The
NORTH SEA
and the
BALTIC SEA

Nina Morgan

RSVP

RAINTREE
STECK-VAUGHN
PUBLISHERS
The Steck-Vaughn Company

Austin, Texas

Seas and Oceans series

The Atlantic Ocean
The Caribbean and the Gulf of Mexico
The Indian Ocean
The Mediterranean Sea
The North Sea and the Baltic Sea
The Pacific Ocean
The Polar Seas
The Red Sea and the Arabian Gulf

Cover: An oil rig in the North Sea

Published by Raintree Steck-Vaughn Publishers, an imprint of Steck-Vaughn Company

Library of Congress Cataloging-in-Publication Data
Morgan, Nina.
The North Sea and the Baltic Sea / Nina Morgan.
    p.   cm.
    Includes bibliographical references and index.
    Summary: Describes the formation, underwater landscape, plant and animal life, natural resources, and pollution of the North and Baltic Seas.
    ISBN 0-8172-4510-3
    1. Oceanography—North Sea—Juvenile literature.
    2. Oceanography—Baltic Sea—Juvenile literature.
    [1. North Sea. 2. Baltic Sea.]
    I. Title.
    GC591.M67 1997
    551.46'136—dc20   96-19443

Printed in Italy. Bound in the United States.
1 2 3 4 5 6 7 8 9 0 01 00 99 98 97

Picture acknowledgments:
Finn G. Andersen 9, 13; Dieter Betz 22; Ecoscene 6–7 (Hulme), 12 (Leeny), 19 (Tweedie); Eye Ubiquitous 17, 28, 31 (Nick Wiseman), 34 (Trip/V. Kolpakov), 37 (Larry Bray), 41 (Niklas Kjeldsen); Frank Lane Picture Agency 40 (Peter Reynolds), 45 (Peter Reynolds); Geoscience Features 4–5, 18, 35 (top), 38–9; Ole Steen Hansen 8, 10, 14, 16, 25, 29, 33 (inset); Life File 20–21 (Ron Williamson), 27 (Andrew Ward), 30 (Malcolm Parker), 33 (bottom/Nigel Sitwell), 39 (inset/Nigel Shuttleworth); Papilio 23; Popperfoto 44; Tony Stone International *cover*, 11 (Marcus Brooke); Topham Picture Point 43; Julia Waterlow 32; Wayland Picture Library 26.
All artwork is supplied by Hardlines except Stephen Chabluk 35 (bottom).

Contents

Words that appear in **bold** in the text can be found in the glossary on page 46.

INTRODUCTION
Contrasting Seas

Although the North Sea and the Baltic Sea are near neighbors, in many ways they are very different. The North Sea is open to the Atlantic Ocean to the north and south and has a normal marine **salinity**. Thanks to a warm current entering from the Atlantic, the North Sea never freezes in the winter. Strong tides and a complicated pattern of currents mean that North Sea waters are well mixed and rich in the nutrients needed to support a varied and abundant collection of plants and animals.

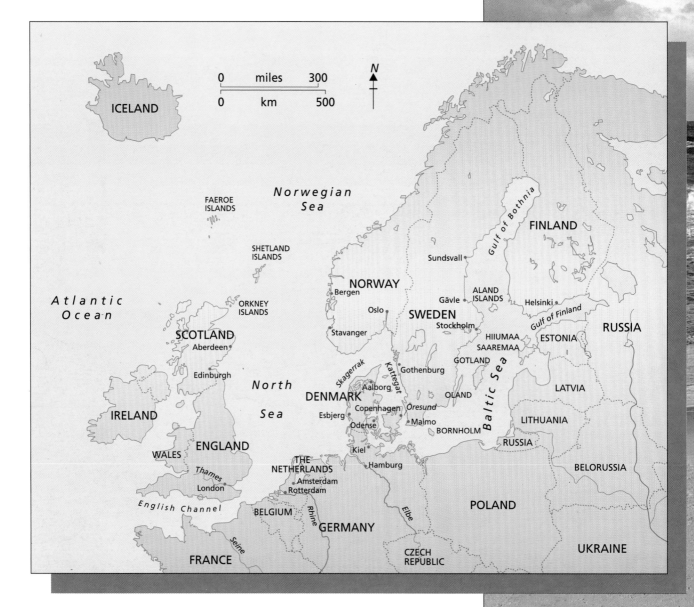

A sandy beach near Kalingrad, Lithuania, on the southern coast of the Baltic near the border with Poland.

In contrast, the Baltic Sea is largely surrounded by land, and connected to the North Sea only by narrow straits between Denmark and Sweden. Because only relatively small amounts of saltwater can pass through this entrance, much of the water entering the Baltic is freshwater from rivers. As a result, Baltic waters are **brackish**. In fact, the Baltic Sea is one of the largest areas of brackish water in the world and is home to very interesting plant and animal communities.

The Baltic experiences few tides. Circulation is slow, and the waters are clearly layered (the layers differ in temperature and salinity), rather than well mixed. With no warm currents coming in, and very low salinities, frozen seas in winter are a fact of life for animals, plants, and people living in many areas around the Baltic Sea.

Left: This map of the North Sea and Baltic region shows the main fringing bodies of water, and some of the islands, cities, and rivers.

But in spite of these differences, the two seas have some features in common. In **geological** terms, the two seas were formed very recently, and in each sea **glaciers** played an important role in its formation. In contrast with oceans such as the Atlantic or the Pacific, which are located on **oceanic crust**, the North Sea and the Baltic Sea are both located in depressions, or low areas, in the crust of the continent of Europe.

In both regions, the sea serves as a major transportation route, and fishing is an important industry. Throughout history, the Baltic and the North Sea have had a strong influence on the lives of those who have lived around them.

THE UNDERWATER LANDSCAPE
A Sea of Change

About 2.5 million years ago, the North Sea was dry land and it was possible to walk between Great Britain and the rest of Europe. The North Sea we know today was created when water from melting ice sheets flooded the land. The last **land bridge** between England and France was submerged just 8,000–9,000 years ago. The coastlines we recognize today were established only about 1,000 years ago.

The North Sea lies in a depression in the continent of Europe that has existed for more than 350 million years. By studying more than 19,000 feet of **sediments** preserved beneath the sea floor in some parts of the North Sea, geologists have discovered much about its history.

During the Carboniferous period, about 360 million years ago, the North Sea was a huge swamp. Later, about 286 million years ago, the sea was surrounded by deserts. In the Jurassic period (about 213–97 million years ago), rivers flowed into the sea and deposited huge triangular-shaped piles of sediments known as deltas. At other times the region was covered first by deeper, clearer water, and then by ice sheets. It was only when the ice melted and moved northward between 13,000 and 8,000 years ago that the North Sea became more like the sea we know today.

Because the sea floor dips to the north, the northern North Sea is generally deeper than the southern part. The seabed is covered by mud, sand, and gravel left behind by glaciers. In parts of the North Sea these glacial deposits have been pushed into heaps by strong currents to form shallow banks. The biggest of these are the Dogger Bank in the southern North Sea and the Jutland Bank off the coast of Denmark.

How big and how deep?		
	North Sea	**Baltic Sea**
Area	220,000 sq. mi.	162,000 sq. mi.
Average depth	300 ft.	200–225 ft.
Shallowest offshore area	50 ft. on the Dogger Bank	26 ft. near Öresund, between Denmark and Sweden
Maximum depth	over 2,400 ft. in the Skagerrak	1,500 ft. in the Landsort Deep

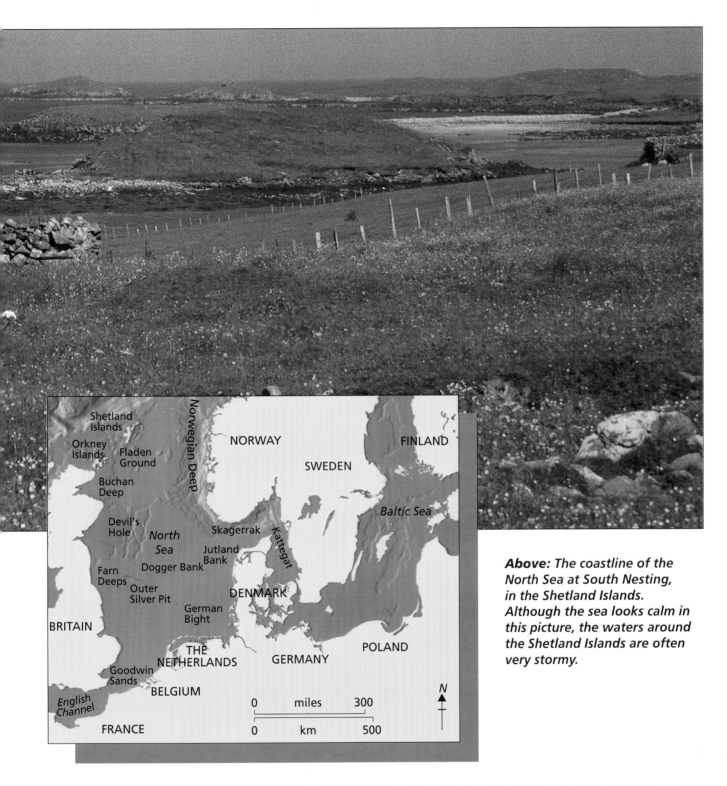

Above: The coastline of the North Sea at South Nesting, in the Shetland Islands. Although the sea looks calm in this picture, the waters around the Shetland Islands are often very stormy.

Above: This map shows the underwater landscape of the North Sea and the Baltic, with its trenches and plains.

In other parts of the North Sea floor, glaciers have cut down old river valleys to form deep **trenches**. One of the largest trenches is the Norwegian Deep, an area 500 miles long and between 15–20 miles wide, which runs parallel to the coast of Norway from north of Bergen to Oslo. In parts of this area the water is more than 2,300 feet deep.

THE UNDERWATER LANDSCAPE
Baltic Ups and Downs

Like the North Sea, the Baltic Sea also formed in a depression in the continent of Europe. By studying fossils preserved in the sediments in parts of the sea, geologists and biologists have been able to show that the water in the Baltic Sea has changed, from freshwater to saltwater and back again, several times during its history.

The Baltic Sea is much younger than the North Sea. It was created only about 10,500 years ago when melting ice sheets retreated northward and left behind a huge freshwater lake. As the glaciers continued to melt, sea levels rose in the North Sea and the land in the Baltic area began to rise as the heavy weight of the ice was removed. Sometimes sea levels rose faster than the land areas, so the Baltic Sea was flooded with saltwater. At other times the land rose more quickly, and the Baltic Sea was isolated from the North Sea and became more like a freshwater lake again.

Below: The rocky coastline of the island of Bornholm in the Baltic. This small island lies off the southern tip of Sweden and is separated from the Swedish mainland by a passage known as Bornholmsgattet.

In some parts of the Baltic Sea the land is still moving. Around the Gulf of Bothnia between Sweden and Finland, the land is rising about .5 inch each year. Meanwhile, in the southern part of the Baltic Sea, the land is sinking about .1 inch per year. As a result, the shape of the Baltic Sea is changing, becoming gradually smaller.

The seabed in the northern part of the Baltic Sea is rocky and made up mainly of "basement" rocks—very old **crystalline** rocks that formed the core of an ancient continent. In some places these rocks are covered by very old sediments laid down more than 550 million years ago. In other parts the deposits are much younger.

Above: White chalk cliffs at the Cliff of Stevns on the west coast of Sjaelland, Denmark. The chalk is formed from the fossilized skeletons of tiny, floating animals, which were deposited in the warm sea that covered this part of Denmark thousands of years ago.

Coastlines and Islands

Today, the North Sea is bordered by Great Britain to the southwest and west, the Orkney and Shetland islands to the northwest, Norway to the northeast, Denmark to the east, Germany and The Netherlands to the southeast, and Belgium and France to the south. It is connected to the Atlantic by the Straits of Dover and the English Channel in the south. In the north the North Sea opens directly into the Atlantic between the Orkney and Shetland islands. The North Sea is connected to the Baltic by an eastward extension called the Skagerrak.

Baltic Islands

The central region of the Baltic is dotted with thousands of islands formed from polished, rocky surfaces or from rocky rubble piled up by the movement of the glaciers. These islands have been slowly rising above the sea level ever since the glaciers retreated. The two largest groups of islands are in the **Archipelago** Sea off the southwest coast of Finland and in the Stockholm archipelago.

The coastline of the North Sea is very variable. Many parts of the North Sea are surrounded by rocky coastlines with steep cliffs. These were formed when the sea cut into the rising land surface around the basin. Along other parts of the

Above: The harbor at Stromness on the Orkney Islands. Fishing is an important industry in these small islands, which are located off the northern tip of Scotland. The Orkneys are separated from the Scottish mainland by a strait known as the Pentland Firth.

Left: Mandø is just one of the many islands lining the southeastern coasts of the North Sea. Low, sandy islands characterize this part of the North Sea coast, which stretches from The Netherlands northward to Germany and Denmark.

coastline, for example, around The Netherlands, the land is slowly sinking and coastal lowlands are forming. Low-lying, sandy areas also form where rivers break through the cliffs to the sea. Islands occur along many North Sea coastlines. Some are rocky, like the small islands that fringe the coast of Norway, or the Shetland and Orkney island groups off the northern coast of Scotland. Others, like the Frisian Islands, a chain of islands off the coast of The Netherlands and northern Germany and Denmark, are small, low, and sandy.

In the southern Baltic the shorelines are often made of flat stretches of sand or small pebbles and are dotted with larger rocks and boulders left behind by the glaciers. The coastline in the north and in the Gulf of Bothnia is more rocky. Along the Swedish Baltic coast, the action of waves and frosts has created cliffs up to 230 feet high. Islands are very common in some parts of the Baltic.

Salinity and Surface Temperatures

Thanks to the North Atlantic Drift, an extension of the Gulf Stream that carries warm water across the Atlantic toward northern Europe, the waters of the North Sea are much warmer than those in other seas located as far north. Although other coastal seas at similar latitudes are generally frozen in the winter, water temperatures in the North Sea remain above the freezing point of seawater.

Temperatures in the Baltic vary greatly throughout the year. In winter, ice may cover parts of the Baltic Sea surface from December to April. In very cold years ice forms along all the Baltic coasts. In the summer the surface water temperatures in sheltered bays and inlets can get quite high.

The salinity of the open North Sea ranges between 34 and 35 parts per thousand, similar to that found in the major oceans. The North Sea is slightly less salty off the coast of Norway thanks to an inflow of fresher water from the Baltic. Freshwater also enters the North Sea from many rivers, such as the Thames in England and the Rhine in Germany.

Right: The Rhine River in Germany is used to carry goods from North Sea ports such as Rotterdam in The Netherlands, to destinations in the interior of Europe. The riverbanks have been lined along many parts of the Rhine to form a canal for shipping. Long narrow boats, or barges, with large decks for carrying cargo, are used to carry goods along the Rhine.

Below: The Thames River in London, England. Fresh water from the Thames drains into the North Sea. The river also provides a gateway to the interior of England.

In contrast, most of the Baltic Sea is not very salty. The salinity of the Baltic waters is very low, because this sea is fed by more than 200 rivers and does not receive much salty water from the North Sea. Any water that does flow in from the North Sea generally sinks to the bottom. As a result, the bottom waters of the Baltic are saltier than the surface layers.

Most seas have layers of water that can be recognized by their different salinity and temperature characteristics. In the Baltic the water layers are very well defined, and the Baltic is often said to be strongly **stratified** because water from different layers cannot mix together very easily. In the Baltic the **halocline**, which separates brackish surface waters from saltier bottom waters, occurs at different depths in different parts of the sea. In the main part of the Baltic the **thermocline**, separating warmer waters from colder ones, develops at a depth of about 98 feet.

	North Sea	Baltic Sea
Average temperatures (winter)	35–46°F	about 32°F
Average temperatures (summer)	54–59°F	50–55°F
Salinity (parts per thousand)	34–35	20 (bottom waters) 10 (western Baltic) 2 (northern Gulf of Bothnia)

Currents

The flow of currents in the North Sea is controlled by the tides, by the direction of the winds, and by **density** differences in the water layers.

The main currents in the North Sea flow in a counterclockwise direction, but near the coasts the current patterns are very complicated. The flow of currents can be very different, depending on the area of the sea and the time of year. The English Channel, for example, has its own set of currents that vary from season to season.

A Breath of Fresh Air

Although some oxygen enters the Baltic surface waters from the atmosphere, most oxygen enters this sea only when westerly winds and high air pressure push heavier, saltier, oxygen-rich water from the North Sea through the Kattegat. Once in the Baltic, this heavier North Sea water sinks and flows toward the central part of the sea, where it replaces oxygen-poor bottom waters. The last major inflow of oxygen into the Baltic took place in the winter of 1992. Using knowledge of past flows, scientists predict that it could be up to 20 years before another major oxygen inflow event occurs.

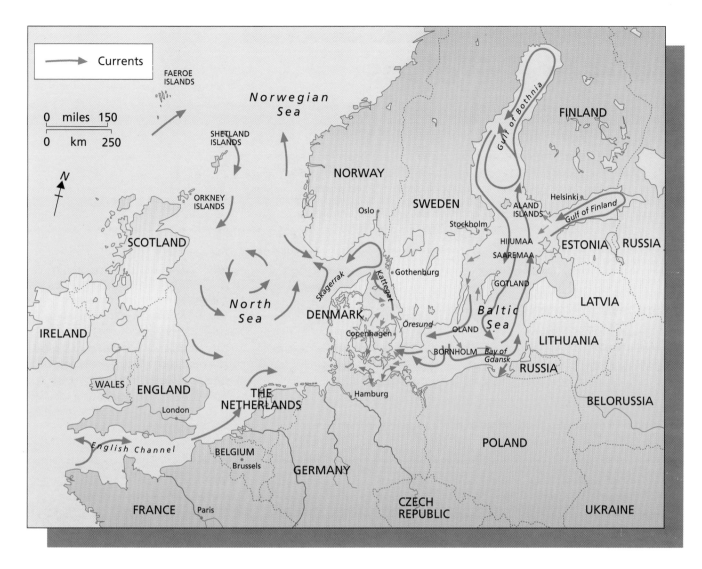

Above: The current patterns of the North Sea and Baltic are very complicated. The surface currents of the region can be seen on this map. Current flow in the region is generated by the tides, by the strongest winds, and by differences in density.

Left: A sailing barge traveling through the Kattegat near Hundested, on the northern shore of the largest Danish island, Sjaelland.

In some parts of the North Sea, including the central and northern areas, currents are not very strong. But in other areas, such as the English Channel, the currents can be powerful enough to push up large banks of sand from the sea floor.

The currents throughout the Baltic are generally not very strong. Like the North Sea, the main pattern of circulation in the Baltic is counterclockwise. Some water does flow into the Baltic from the North Sea through the Skagerrak and the Kattegat, but because these straits are narrow and shallow, this flow of water is very slow. This means that water in the Baltic is completely replaced only once every 25–50 years.

With no new oxygen-rich waters flowing in, oxygen levels in parts of the Baltic are very low. As a result, some areas of the Baltic seabed support very little life.

Tides and Storms

The Baltic Sea experiences few tides, but in the North Sea tides are very important. The pattern of North Sea tides is very complicated because Great Britain acts as a barrier to the flow of water from the Atlantic. The rising tides from the Atlantic enter the North Sea in two waves, one coming from the southwest and the other from the north. These two tidal waves reach any given point in the North Sea at different times, so sometimes they work together and sometimes they cancel each other out. As a result, the **tidal ranges** vary greatly around North Sea coasts.

Along much of the coast of Norway, tidal ranges are often less than 3 feet. In contrast, the tidal ranges along the east coast of Britain can be up to 18 feet. The range can be even greater—in the Bay of Mont-St.-Michel, on the French side of the English Channel, 27.5-feet tidal ranges are common.

Below: The rough seas and winter storms mean that even today shipwrecks are not uncommon in the busy shipping routes around the North Sea and the Baltic. This ship ran aground in the North Sea off the west coast of Denmark during a storm in 1995.

Tidal currents can be very strong in the North Sea. For example, the flow of water due to the tides is more than six m.p.h. off the Cherbourg **peninsula** in France and Portland Bill, on the Portland peninsula in southeast England.

Both the North Sea and the Baltic Sea can be very stormy, with large, dangerous waves whipped up by strong winds. In the Baltic Sea, strong northeasterly winds often create high waves along the southern shores. These can cause flooding along the coast. In the northern North Sea, winds that are almost hurricane strength and 82-feet high waves have been known to occur during the frequent winter gales. No wonder the Romans thought of the North Sea as the roughest sea in the world.

Above: When the tide is out, it is possible to walk from the mainland to the island of Mont-St.-Michel, on the French side of the English Channel. For hundreds of years, the church on this island has been a popular destination for both pilgrims and tourists.

Plants and Invertebrates

The nutrient-rich marine waters in the North Sea support a huge variety of plant and invertebrate species. The rocky coastlines, sandy and muddy shores, and sea bottom of the North Sea are home to a wealth of marine plants. These include red and green seaweeds, as well as brown seaweeds such as kelp, single-celled algae, and eel grass. All these plants play an important role in the lives of many types of **invertebrates**. Among these are snails, such as periwinkles, which use rasping tongues to graze on the surface film that covers the seaweeds.

The seabed in the North Sea is home to many other invertebrates, for example, **bivalves** such as scallops, cockles, and mussels. On muddy bottoms, the cockles may bury themselves below the surface. Mussels live attached to the surfaces of rocks. Scallops live freely on the surface and can swim around. These animals live by filtering food particles out of the water. They send up a **siphon** to carry in and send out water containing oxygen and food particles to and from their gills.

Below: Shellfish such as mussels, limpets, and barnacles firmly attach themselves to rocks along the coastline where they filter their food out of the water. When the tide is low, these animals withdraw into their shells to stop themselves from drying out.

Seaweeds are also important plants in the Baltic Sea. Many types of red, brown, and green seaweeds live along rocky coastlines in the Kattegat, the most marine, or salty, area of the Baltic. In sheltered, less salty areas of the Baltic, seaweeds known as bladderwrack form underwater forests. There are several species of bladderwracks, and each can survive in different levels of salinity.

In the more marine areas of the bladderwrack zone, great colonies of mussels form dense mats on the rocks. In the less salty areas, freshwater worms, sponges, and snails are common. The bladderwrack community supports 50 different species of plants and animals—half are marine and half are freshwater. This mixture of freshwater and marine organisms living together is widespread in the Baltic Sea.

Above: Bladderwrack seaweeds are common in rock pools around the Baltic. Bladderwrack is well adapted to this environment because it can survive exposure to air and changes in salinity.

Fish

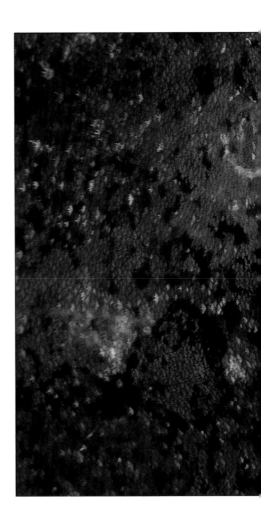

More than 170 species of fish live in the well-mixed and nutrient-rich waters of the North Sea. The variety is amazing. There are primitive, jawless fish, such as lampreys and hagfish; there are sharks and rays, which have skeletons made of **cartilage** rather than of bone; and many different types of true bony fish. These include herring and mackerel, which swim near the surface, and haddock, cod, and saithe, which live near the seabed. There are also flatfish, including flounder, plaice, and sole. These fish have both eyes on one side of their heads and swim on the other side. This makes them specially adapted for life on the sea floor.

In the Baltic Sea, freshwater fish such as sticklebacks, roach, bleak, ruffe, bream, pike, perch, sea trout, and rudd mix with marine fish such as gobies, bullheads, butterfish, and flounders.

One of the most widespread fish species in the Baltic is the herring. This type of fish has **evolved** a number of different subspecies and local races. The Atlantic subspecies occurs throughout the North Sea and enters just the western part of the Baltic. There is also a separate Baltic subspecies. Some types live only around the coasts, while others, known as sea herrings, range from coast to coast in the central Baltic Sea.

There are other fish in the Baltic Sea, such as cod, which have evolved to live under the difficult conditions of the Baltic environment. Of the flatfish, flounder are the most common because their bodies are better equipped to survive the brackish conditions.

Surviving in the Baltic

Both freshwater and marine organisms live in the brackish waters of the Baltic, but neither finds life very easy. Here the concentration of salts in the bodies of marine organisms is much greater than in the water. The salt in their bodies attracts the water in a process called **osmosis**. As a result, the water floods into their bodies. Freshwater species face the opposite problem—water flows out of their bodies. To survive, the organisms must be able to control the flow of water in and out of their bodies. Not all species can manage this, and those that can must use extra energy just to stay alive.

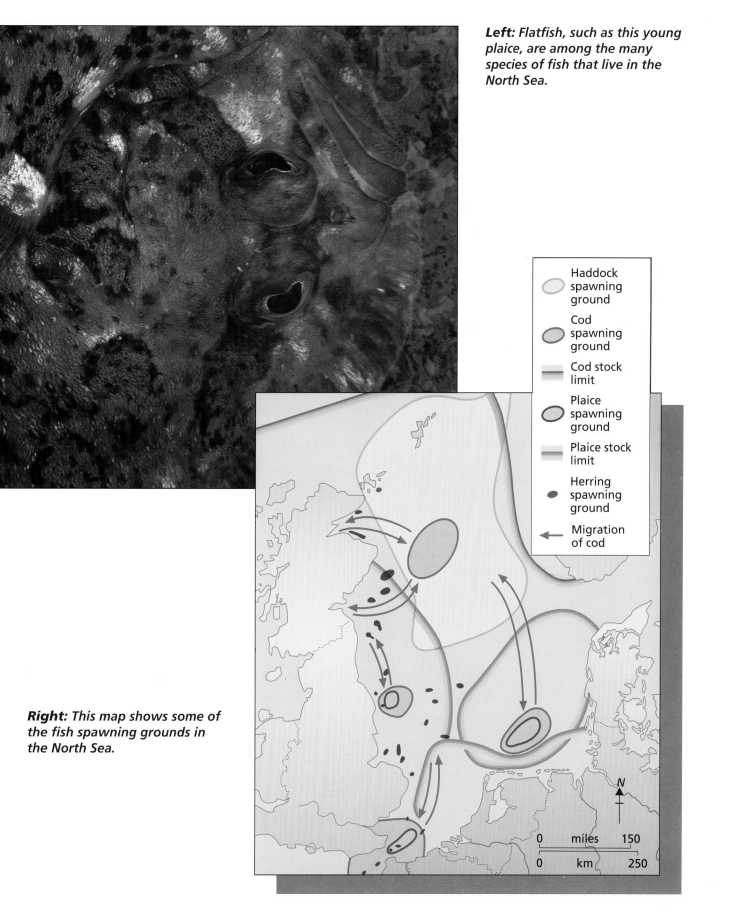

Left: *Flatfish, such as this young plaice, are among the many species of fish that live in the North Sea.*

Haddock spawning ground

Cod spawning ground

Cod stock limit

Plaice spawning ground

Plaice stock limit

Herring spawning ground

Migration of cod

Right: *This map shows some of the fish spawning grounds in the North Sea.*

N

0	miles	150
0	km	250

Birds and Mammals

The rich fishing in the North Sea attracts huge numbers of birds. Some, including guillemots, razorbills, puffins, gannets, kittiwakes, terns, and fulmars, breed on the cliffs along northern North Sea coasts. Other birds, such as cormorants, shags, and gulls, along with ducks such as mergansers, goosanders, shelducks, and eiders, often feed in coastal waters.

Gulls are very common in both seas, but many other sea birds, including gannets, puffins, fulmars, and shags, do not live in the Baltic Sea because they need access to the open ocean. In both the North Sea and the Baltic, large numbers of waders, including sandpipers, curlews, and oystercatchers, feed along the shore.

Gray seals and harbor seals live and breed in both the North Sea and the Baltic. A third species, the ringed seal, is found only in the Gulf of Bothnia and the Gulf of Finland in the Baltic. Although there are still many seals in both seas, there are signs that the seal population is threatened, especially in the Baltic. A virus killed thousands of harbor seals in the North Sea and the Baltic in 1988. Scientists are now worried that pollution in the Baltic Sea may affect the health of the seals there.

Right: A pair of puffins survey the scene along the northern coast of the North Sea. Rich fishing and access to the open ocean waters attract large numbers of puffins and other sea birds to the North Sea.

Several types of dolphins and whales live in the North Sea. The largest of the marine mammals is the Orca, or killer whale. This animal can grow up to 30 feet long and lives by eating fish, seals, and even common porpoises. Common, bottlenose, Risso's, and white-beaked dolphins are also found in parts of the North Sea.

Minke and fin whales, which feed mainly on herrings, were once very common in the North Sea. Now they are harder to find. Baleen whales, which feed by straining **plankton** out of the sea, are also seen in the North Sea.

Above: Dolphins, such as this bottlenose dolphin, are found in the North Sea.

A Way of Life

The sea has always played an important role in the lives of people living in the Baltic region. The earliest settlements were on the coast. When the first Stone Age hunter-gatherers arrived in the area 8,000 years ago, the sea provided them with food. Later, the sea became the most important means of transportation for both people and goods, until the coming of the railroads in the late 1800s.

Fishing is still an important source of income for many people who live around the Baltic, and the sea is still an important means of transportation. Ferry routes crisscross the Baltic Sea, taking passengers and cars between ports in Finland, Sweden, Russia, Latvia, Estonia, Poland, Germany, and Denmark.

Below: On this map you can see the various ferry routes and ports found in the North Sea and Baltic Sea. Ferries are a very popular form of transportation in this region.

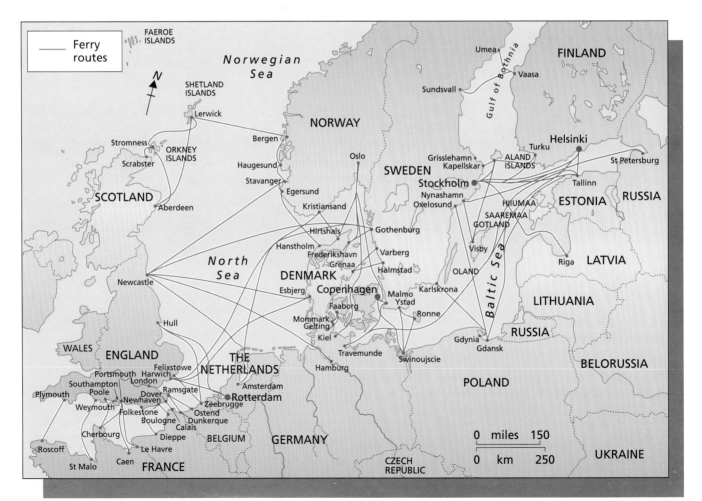

24

Right: The bow doors open wide to allow cars to drive into the car decks on the large drive-on, drive-off ferries. This Swedish ferry is typical of the larger car ferries seen in the Baltic.

Huge, luxurious ferries travel between Finland and Sweden several times each day. Helsinki in Finland is one of the ferry capitals of the world, with many large ferries leaving and arriving every day to and from destinations in Sweden, Estonia, and Poland.

The North Sea, too, has always had a strong influence on the people who live around it and provided an important highway for trade. Today, ferries are a common way of traveling in the North Sea. An extensive network of ferry routes allows people to travel easily between Great Britain, Norway, Sweden, Denmark, The Netherlands, and France. In 1995, travelers between Great Britain and France were offered a new option for crossing the sea—the Channel Tunnel—a railroad tunnel that extends for 31 miles beneath the English Channel between Cheriton, England, and Sangatte, France.

The North Sea and the Baltic Sea have also provided many people with a way of making their living. Fishing has long been important in both regions. Countries bordering both seas are well known for their shipbuilding industries.

Shipbuilding

Although the shipbuilding industries are not as large as they once were, partly due to competition from shipyards in the Far East, there are still many big shipyards in the North Sea and Baltic areas. These yards build many different types of ships for use all over the world.

One of the largest shipbuilders in the Baltic, the Finnish-Norwegian company Kvaerner Masa-Yards, has shipyards in Turku in southwestern Finland and in the Finnish capital and port city, Helsinki. Kvaerner Masa-Yards build a wide variety of ships, ranging from cruise liners and ferries, to tankers for carrying

The Offshore Industry

As North Sea oil production expanded in the early 1970s, the offshore oil industry needed rigs, production platforms, and support vessels to help find, recover, and bring the oil and gas back to shore. This offered new opportunities for offshore engineering companies located around the North Sea in countries such as Great Britain, The Netherlands, and Norway. During the "boom" times in the late 1970s, 1980s, and early 1990s, when many new fields were being developed, offshore engineering companies had lots of orders. But when the oil companies were developing fewer fields, work was harder to find, and some yards were forced to close.

Above: *With the decline in demand for new ships, many North Sea shipyards began building offshore structures for use in the North Sea oilfields. Here, an oil platform is shown under construction at a yard in Gothenburg, Sweden. Gothenburg, located on the Skagerrak, with easy access to the North Sea, is Sweden's largest port.*

Left: *Much of the oil from North Sea oilfields is transported to the shore via underwater pipelines, but some is carried to refineries and storage areas by oil tankers such as this one.*

liquefied natural gas, and sophisticated icebreakers. The icebreakers are used in the Arctic to keep shipping channels open during the Baltic winter.

Other major Baltic shipyards include the Danish yard B&W Skibsvaerft in Copenhagen and the HDW Yard in Kiel, Germany. There are also several large shipyards on the Baltic coast of Poland.

In the North Sea, one of the biggest of the shipbuilders is the Norwegian Ulstein Yard, located in Ålesund, north of Bergen. The Ulstein Yard is a major builder of the **supply vessels** that are used by the oil industry. Another important shipbuilder in the North Sea is Danyard, at Frederikshavn in Denmark. British shipyards along the North Sea coasts were once very large, but these yards are now declining in importance.

Cities by the Sea

In the countries surrounding the North Sea and the Baltic, some of the most important industrial centers are also port cities. Rotterdam, on the North Sea coast of The Netherlands, is now the largest port in the world and Europe's leading container terminal. This modern city, which was largely rebuilt after World War II, is also a center for manufacturing, shipbuilding, and oil refining. The port of Rotterdam is one of the best equipped in the world, with special cranes available to lift huge containers and place them directly into a ship's hold or onto a truck or railroad car.

Hamburg, in Germany, which is located on the Elbe River about 70 miles from where the river drains into the North Sea, is another important North Sea port. Hamburg is Germany's second largest city, and its busy port plays a very important part in the city's economy. Much of the oil, iron ore, copper, wheat, wool, cotton, and hides that serve as raw materials for the city's industries are brought in by sea.

In the Baltic, Helsinki is the capital and main manufacturing center of Finland. This busy port handles more than half of all Finland's foreign trade. It is also home to important

Right: The famous B&W Skibsvaerft shipyards in Copenhagen, Denmark, are located on the island in the center of the picture. The large tanks are for storing oil.

Below: The Swedish capital, Stockholm, is a city of canals. Ferries, such as the one shown here, are a common means of transportation around the city. The ferries also carry passengers to other Baltic ports.

engineering and shipbuilding industries, and to food- and timber-processing plants. This pleasant city, largely rebuilt in the nineteenth century after a serious fire, is also the cultural and educational center of Finland.

Stockholm, located on Sweden's Baltic coast, is the capital city of Sweden and the country's chief manufacturing center. It is also Sweden's second-largest port. Only Gothenburg on the North Sea coast is larger. Stockholm is a city of canals and is often called "the Venice of the North." People in Stockholm are well used to traveling by ferry to reach different parts of the city, and a number of bridges have been built to link various districts.

The Danish capital, Copenhagen, has always played a special role in sea travel because it is located at the southern end of the Öresund, the waterway that separates Denmark from Sweden and links the Baltic with the North Sea. Today, Copenhagen is the largest city in Scandinavia. It is among the cities most visited by tourists, who delight in the narrow winding streets of the old city and enjoy visiting the harbor and canals. It is also the largest manufacturing center in Denmark.

Number of goods handled at major North Sea and Baltic ports per year

Rotterdam 282 million tons of cargo, including containers

Helsinki 8 million tons of cargo; 280,000 20 feet-container units; 1,650,000 trucks and trailers; 6.3 million passengers

Stockholm 4.8 million tons of cargo; 7.6 million passengers

Copenhagen 9.4 million tons of cargo; 146,868 20 feet-container units

Hamburg 64 million tons of cargo, including containers and petroleum

Traffic Jams and Bad Weather

The North Sea and the Baltic Sea include some of the busiest shipping routes in the world, although natural conditions in both seas can sometimes make shipping very dangerous.

The North Sea is an important transportation route for distributing **raw materials** and finished goods around the industrial centers of northern Europe and throughout the world. There are nearly half a million voyages every year in the southern North Sea alone.

By 1967 the sea traffic in the Dover Strait had become so heavy that shipping lanes were established to separate ships traveling east from those traveling west. Now a complicated set of shipping routes exists in the North Sea to help ships weave their way through oil

Containerization

Many cargoes are now packed into containers that travel to and from ports, on trucks, or by railroad. At the ports special cranes are used to load the containers directly into the holds of purpose-built container ships. The containers come in standard sizes and can be heated, refrigerated, ventilated, or specially fitted to carry different types of goods. The use of containers speeds handling at ports because container ships can be quickly loaded and unloaded. With other types of cargo vessels it normally takes about one hour to load 10 tons of cargo. In contrast, a 34-ton container can be loaded or unloaded from a container ship in just 10 minutes.

Left: These icebreakers, tied up in the harbor at Stockholm, Sweden, have heavy bows that are specially designed to break up and travel through the ice that covers large parts of the Gulf of Bothnia in winter. They can also be used in open waters.

and gas fields, fishing grounds, sand- and gravel-extraction sites, and military exercise zones. Even so, accidents still occur when ships ignore the lanes.

Natural conditions such as drifting sandbanks, strong tides, and frequent winter storms also make this busy shipping area more dangerous. Sunken wrecks are another hazard. There are more than 14,000 wrecks in the North Sea off the coast of Great Britain alone. To keep ships informed about the location of dangerous areas, the main shipping lanes in the English Channel are regularly monitored to note the changing position of sandbanks and other hazards.

Natural hazards also affect shipping in the Baltic. One of the biggest problems is sailing through icy seas and bad weather in the winter. In the Gulf of Bothnia the sea freezes every winter, and icebreakers are used to keep channels and ports open in both Sweden and Finland. Icebreakers are especially important to Finnish shipping, because Finland is the only country in the world where all the ports are frozen every winter.

Above: Although the harbor in Helsinki, Finland, freezes nearly every winter, it remains open to shipping throughout the year. Icebreakers break up the ice in winter and make it possible for other ships to enter the harbor.

Canals

Until the end of the nineteenth century, ships traveling between the Baltic and the North Sea had no option but to pass through the shallow and narrow straits of the Öresund and the Kattegat. This posed a great danger, especially for large ships. The problem was solved in 1895, with the opening of the Kiel Canal.

The Kiel Canal was originally built in 1887 for use by German military ships. It was widened in 1907 and 1914, so the canal could be used largely by commercial merchant ships. The canal extends 61 miles across the northern peninsula of Germany, from Kiel on the Baltic coast to Brunsbüttel on the North Sea coast. It is crossed by seven high-level bridges.

The Kiel Canal is 338 feet wide and 36 feet deep. It can be used by ships up to 131 feet wide, which can float in less than 30 feet of water. Although the canal is at sea level, it is separated from the Baltic and the North Sea by a system of locks. These prevent water in the canal from rising and falling with the North Sea tides.

The average travel time through the Kiel Canal is seven hours. Depending on the route, using the canal shortens the

Below: A Greek tanker traveling along the Kiel Canal

journey between the Baltic and the North Sea by up to 31 miles. The Kiel Canal is one of the busiest in the world—more than 90,000 ships pass through it every year. It is especially used by smaller cargo boats and coastal boats.

Canals are important in other parts of the North Sea too. Inland canals along rivers such as the Rhine and the Meuse provide important access to the North Sea from the interior of Europe. Cargo from the center of Europe is carried along these canals to ports such as Rotterdam, where it is transferred onto ocean-going ships. This system means that ports like Rotterdam can serve as a worldwide gateway to many inland industrial centers in northern Europe.

Below: *Charming houses along the canals in the Danish capital, Copenhagen, are popular with tourists and residents alike.*

Below: *Canals offer important gateways to inland centers in Europe and Scandinavia from both the North Sea and the Baltic. The Gotä Canal, shown here, runs between Gothenburg on the west coast of Sweden to the city of Vänersborg on the shores of Lake Vänern in south-central Sweden.*

Fish: A Living Resource

Although the North Sea makes up just 0.2 percent of all the world's oceans, it is the source of more than 5 percent of the fish caught worldwide. About 2–3 tons of fish per square mile are caught there each year. Fish are so abundant in the North Sea because the well-mixed, nutrient-rich waters contain large amounts of plankton, which many of the fish feed on.

In the North Sea, herring, mackerel, and whiting, along with the bottom-dwelling fish such as plaice, sole, cod, haddock, coley, and turbot, are the most important commercial fish. These are mostly eaten fresh or canned. Some shellfish are also caught.

The Baltic, too, is a major fishing area where commercial fishing boats bring in about a ton of fish per square mile every year. However, there are less fish and fewer species in the Baltic than in the North Sea because the lower salinities and poorly mixed waters make the Baltic a difficult environment

Conserving Fish Stocks

Overfishing is a big problem. If too many fish are caught, not enough are left to breed. In order to conserve fish stocks, fishing nations must protect young fish by setting limits on the minimum size of fish that can be caught. They must also set a **quota** on the numbers of fish of each species that can be caught. The Baltic nations took these steps in 1973. The North Sea nations made a similar agreement in 1983. But these quotas are difficult to set up and to enforce—so progress toward saving fish stocks is slow.

Left: Latvian fishermen with boxes of Baltic herring. Nets are used to catch these small fish, which are brought to shore packed in ice. Herring, either fresh, smoked, or served in a variety of sauces, is a popular food throughout Scandinavia.

in which to live. The conditions in the Baltic also mean that individual fish tend to be much smaller.

In the Baltic, herring, sprats, cod, and flounder are the most important commercial fish in the marine areas. In the brackish areas, perch and vendace are the main catches. Salmon is caught both in the open sea and around river mouths. Of the North Sea countries, Denmark is the main fishing nation, followed by Norway, Great Britain, The Netherlands, France, Germany, and Belgium. Other countries, such as Spain, also fish in North Sea waters. Denmark is also one of the most important fishing nations in the Baltic, along with Finland, Poland, Sweden, and the states of the former Soviet Union.

Below: These small fishing boats are typical of the boats seen in the Baltic Sea.

Below: Different fishing methods are used to catch different types of fish. Trawl nets that are pulled along the seabed are used to catch some bottom-dwelling species. Other types of bottom-dwelling fish are caught using long lines and hooks. Purse-seine nets are used to trap schools of fish swimming near the surface. Surface swimmers are also caught using drift nets, which hang like curtains from floats on the sea surface.

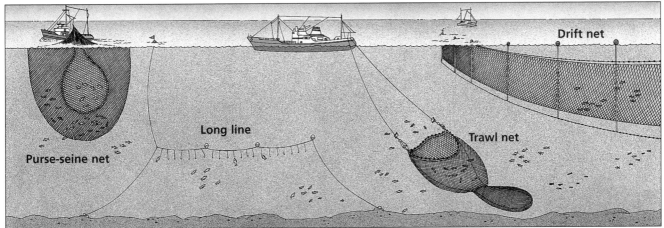

Purse-seine net

Long line

Trawl net

Drift net

RICH RESOURCES
Oil and Gas: The North Sea Bonanza

The sediments of the North Sea are rich in both oil and gas, which formed over millions of years when the remains of plants and animals were buried beneath rocks and "cooked," or chemically changed, at high temperatures and pressures. Oil is found mainly in the northern part of the North Sea, in marine sediments laid down about 150 million years ago. The biggest oil fields are located in British and Norwegian waters. Gas, generated from coal deposited about 300 million years ago, is more common in the southern North Sea. The main gas fields are located off the coast of southern England and The Netherlands.

The search for oil and gas in the North Sea began in 1959. In the mid-1960s the countries surrounding the North Sea agreed to divide up sea floor territory into British, Norwegian, Danish, German, Dutch, Belgian, and French sectors. Each country was allowed to control oil exploration in its sector.

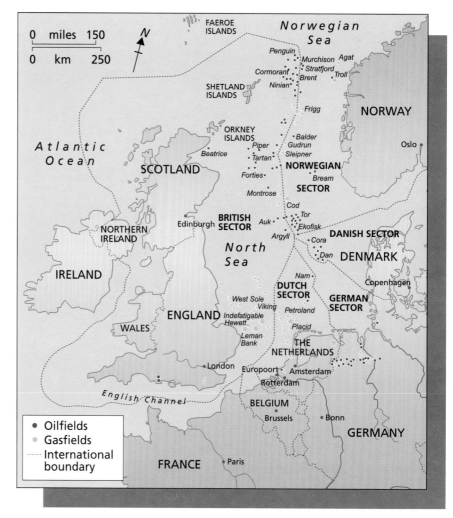

Right: Oil and gas resources are very important in the North Sea region. The major oil and gas fields in the North Sea are represented on this map.

The first big gas field, the West Sole field in the southern North Sea, was discovered in 1965. The first big oil field, the Forties field in the northern North Sea, was found in 1970. By the end of 1993, 110 fields were producing more than 98 million tons of oil and more than 200 billion cubic feet of gas from the British sector alone. There were also about 60 platforms producing oil and gas in the Dutch, Norwegian, Danish, and German sectors. Today, North Sea oil and gas supply about 30 percent of the energy needs of the countries around the North Sea. Some countries, such as Great Britain, get all the oil and gas they need from North Sea fields, and expect to be able to do so well into the next century.

Above: A semisubmersible oil rig exploring for oil and gas in the North Sea. This type of oil rig has large floats below the water level to keep it afloat and is held in position by anchors on the sea floor.

North Sea oil and gas production (in 1993)		
	Oil (barrels per day)	Gas (cu. ft. per year)
Norway	2,375,000	100 billion
Great Britain	2,016,000	260 billion
Denmark	170,000	18 billion
The Netherlands	65,000	336 billion

The North Sea fields are explored and developed by a large group of international oil companies. Some of these companies, such as British Petroleum (BP), the Norwegian company Statoil, and the Dutch company Shell, are based in North Sea countries. Many others, including Esso, Conoco, and Texaco, have their main offices in the United States.

RICH RESOURCES
Sand, Gravel, and Other Minerals

More sand and gravel are gathered from the North Sea than from any other sea in the world. The largest sand and gravel deposits occur off the east coast of Britain. Around 24.5 million tons of gravel are mined here every year for use in concrete and in road surfacing. Sand reserves are even greater. The construction industry is the biggest customer for this resource.

Most of the North Sea gravel was left behind by melting glaciers during the last Ice Age, between 2 million and 10,000 years ago. Later, more sand and gravel were deposited at the mouths of rivers draining into the North Sea. The strong tides and currents in the North Sea mean that the sand and gravel deposits are constantly shifting. In some areas they are being deposited, while in other areas they are being carried away.

The sand and gravel are mined using special boats known as suction dredgers. These boats can only work in water less than 115 feet deep and in areas no more than 75 miles from the shore for safety reasons. The dredgers suck up the sand and gravel using large pipes that reach down to the sea floor. Some dredgers also have trailing pipes that allow them to suck up gravel while the boat is moving forward.

Other minerals now being mined in the North Sea include coal and lime. The coal seams, which extend more than four miles offshore from coal fields in northern England, are worked as part of the mines on land. The lime deposits are mined from the seabed and used on farms in France and Germany.

In the Baltic Sea, amber, or fossilized tree resin, is the most important mineral resource. Amber is mined from greenish sands along the shores of the Baltic. It is also collected from beaches where it has been washed ashore. Amber has been an important source of wealth around the Baltic Sea for nearly 4,000 years.

Left: *A dredger uses a mechanical grab to dredge up accumulated sand and mud. This is to keep the harbor clear for shipping at South Shields, on the west coast of the North Sea in northern England.*

Below: *Amber is still collected from the sea in parts of the Baltic. Here, Russian amber collectors use shrimping nets to gather amber from the **surf zone**. They are wearing wetsuits to protect them from the cold air and water.*

Nutrients: Too Much of a Good Thing?

On land, fertilizers containing nutrients, such as nitrogen and phosphorus, help plants grow. But when large amounts of nutrients wash into the sea, they set off a chain of events known as **eutrophication**. This process stimulates fast growth, or blooms, of tiny plants known as algae. When these masses of algae die, they sink and **decompose**. The decomposition causes oxygen levels to fall sharply near the sea floor, and as a result animals living on the sea bottom die.

Eutrophication is a very serious problem in the Baltic Sea because the water mixes slowly, making it difficult for new oxygen to reach the bottom. The first signs of eutrophication

Left: A layer of algae appears from time to time and covers parts of the sea surface in both the Baltic and the North Sea. Although these blooms can occur naturally, they are often stimulated by excess nutrients washed in from surrounding land areas.

in the Baltic appeared in 1950. By the early 1990s it was estimated that at least 1 million tons of nitrogen and 49,000 tons of phosphorus, mainly from fertilizers used on farms, in forests, and from sewage, were entering the Baltic each year. Although the Baltic nations have agreed to reduce the amount of nutrients that flow into the sea by 50 percent, scientists estimate that it will take between 60 and 100 years to undo the damage already caused.

Too many nutrients also cause problems in the North Sea. Here many of the excess nutrients come from chemical fertilizers washed in from farmers' fields and from poorly treated sewage. In addition, large amounts of nitrogen enter the sea from the atmosphere. The nitrogen comes from the exhausts of cars and trucks and from the burning of **fossil fuels** such as gas, coal, and oil in power stations.

These excess nutrients often lead to algal blooms. In 1988 a massive bloom of algae stretched for 620 miles along the coasts of Denmark and Norway. The algae covered the sea surface and released poisons that killed many marine animals.

Above: The chemical fertilizers used by farmers on their fields are a major source of excess nutrients pouring into the North Sea and the Baltic. Countries surrounding both seas are working to find ways to reduce this nutrient runoff.

THE POLLUTION PROBLEM
Chemicals and Oil

When the oil tanker *Braer* ran aground off the coast of the Shetland Islands in January 1993, spilling 83,000 tons of crude oil into the North Sea, many people were worried that it would cause a major ecological disaster. Yet every year ships in the North Sea release a similar amount of oil when cleaning out their tanks.

Major oil spills that wash ashore kill the sea life on rocky stretches, and the oil can be absorbed into the sand and mud along the shore where it can kill or injure animals that live there. Some marine animals are very sensitive to oil, so even small amounts of oil in the water can harm them.

Below: It is important that we try to control the amount of pollution that finds its way into the sea. This map shows some of the pollution "hot spots" of the North Sea and Baltic.

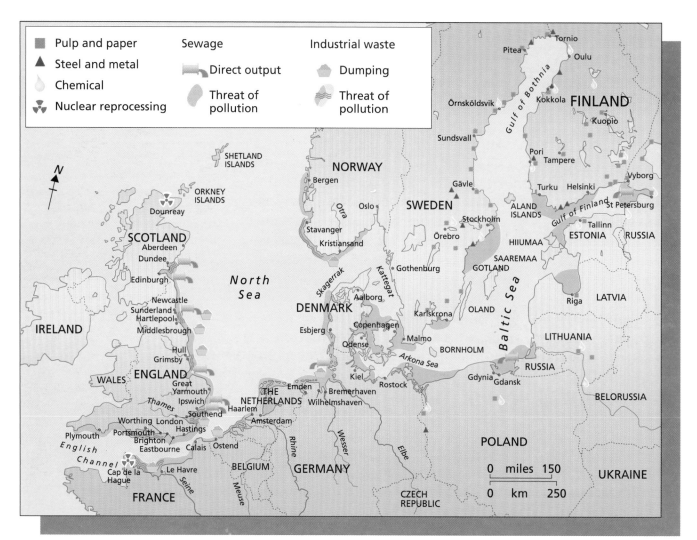

Legend:
- Pulp and paper
- Steel and metal
- Chemical
- Nuclear reprocessing

Sewage
- Direct output
- Threat of pollution

Industrial waste
- Dumping
- Threat of pollution

Because of its large oil industry, the North Sea is most at risk. But oil pollution is also a problem in the Baltic because there are oil refineries along some coasts and large amounts of oil are transported by sea. As a result of these activities, between 20,000 and 65,000 tons of oil went into the Baltic every year between 1980 and 1985. Although the oil companies generally work hard to prevent damage to the environment from oil pollution, accidents do happen, and environmental groups argue that the oil companies could do more to avoid polluting the sea.

Other chemicals entering the sea also cause pollution. Industries around both regions release thousands of tons of heavy metals such as mercury, cadmium, and lead. These metals are carried into the seas by the wind from industrial smokestacks or flow into the seas from polluted rivers. Many of the metal particles settle in the sediments of the sea floor, where some of them are eaten by animals.

Chemicals, such as **halogenated hydrocarbons**, which are used to make products as varied as plastics and **pesticides**, cause an even bigger problem. Many of these do not break down easily. This means they can build up in the bodies of sea animals and through the food chain, posing a threat both to the animals and to the people who eat them.

Right: In 1988 an explosion on the oil rig Piper Alpha *killed more than 100 people and released large amounts of oil into the sea.*

Saving the Seas

In spite of all the pollution problems in the North Sea and the Baltic Sea, it is still not too late to save the seas if action is taken soon. Environmental organizations, scientists, and governments are working in both regions to bring pollution problems to people's attention.

There are some signs that their hard work is beginning to pay off. The eight countries bordering the North Sea have so far held four ministerial conferences to look at ways of tackling pollution. In the first conference, held in 1984 in Bremen, Germany, German delegates established the idea of the Precautionary Principle. This principle states that if we do not know what damage will be done by dumping something into the sea, we should not take any risks and should forbid dumping.

The Bremen meeting was followed by a conference held in London, England, in 1987 and another one in The Hague, The Netherlands, in 1990. At the Hague conference, ministers

Below: The environmental group Greenpeace protested against the dumping of the Brent Spar oil platform in the North Sea, in May 1995.

from North Sea nations committed themselves to reducing many types of pollutants by 50 percent by 1995. The ministers met again in Esbjerg, Denmark, in 1995 to examine how successful their 1990 resolutions had been.

In 1974, the Baltic nations set up a similar type of ministerial organization, known as the Helsinki Commission, to monitor the health of the Baltic. Among other things, the Helsinki Commission sets up projects to help governments around the Baltic establish practical programs to reduce the amount of pollution that flows into the sea.

Many of these practical programs are now being put into effect. Although hope for saving the Baltic Sea is growing, Baltic nations realize that much work is still needed to save their sea.

Above: When oil reaches the shore, it forms a sticky black deposit on beaches, which must be cleaned up to make the areas safe for people, animals, and plants.

Glossary

archipelago A group of small islands.

bivalves Animals such as mussels and clams that live inside a pair of shells.

brackish Water that is a little salty, but not as salty as normal seawater.

cartilage A firm, bendable type of tissue that is present instead of bone in the skeletons of some types of fish.

crystalline A material that is made up of a regular arrangement of atoms or molecules.

decompose To decay or break down into simpler parts.

density The quality of being closely packed or thick.

eutrophication A process that leads to low levels of oxygen and to the death of many forms of sea life. Eutrophication occurs when large amounts of marine plants, known as algae, die and sink to the sea floor. There, decomposing bacteria break down the algae, but at the same time use up the oxygen in the seawater.

evolved Slowly changed over time.

fossil fuels Fuels such as oil, gas, and coal, which were formed when the bodies of ancient plants and animals were buried and heated over millions of years.

geological Having to do with the study of the earth.

glaciers Thick, slowly moving sheets of ice that once covered large parts of the earth's surface. Glaciers are still found in the Arctic and Antarctic and in high mountain ranges such as the Alps.

halocline A distinct layer of seawater that separates lighter, less salty water from denser, saltier water below.

halogenated hydrocarbons A group of artificial chemicals that are used in many different types of products. They can be poisonous to sea life.

invertebrates Animals without backbones.

land bridge A thin strip of land that crosses a body of water and connects two larger areas of land.

oceanic crust A thinner, denser type of crust found commonly under oceans.

osmosis The process that occurs when water passes through a membrane such as skin, from an area of low salt concentration to one of higher salt concentration. Organisms living in such an area have to be able to pump out excess water, and this demands a lot of energy.

peninsula A long piece of land that is surrounded on three sides by water.

pesticides Chemicals used to control pest animals.

plankton Tiny plants and animals that float in the surface waters of the sea.

quota A regulated limit on, for example, how many fish can be caught, or how many goods can be shipped.

raw materials Basic materials that are used to make something else.

salinity The saltiness of seawater. It is measured in parts per thousand.

sediments Particles of sand, mud, or shell fragments that settle on the sea floor or are carried into the sea by rivers or run off from the land.

siphon A tube that can be used to suck in liquids or to squirt them out. Some bivalves live below the sea floor and use a siphon to suck in water to get oxygen and food particles.

stratified Strongly layered.

supply vessels Ships that travel to and from oil platforms and drilling rigs to supply them with the materials they need and to bring food and other supplies to the people working on them.

surf zone The area between where the first waves break and the land.

thermocline A distinct layer of seawater that separates warmer, shallower water from colder, deeper water.

tidal ranges The differences in height between successive high and low waters.

trenches Deep valleys in the sea floor.

Further Information

Books to read:

Baines, John D. *Protecting the Oceans.* Conserving Our World. Milwaukee: Raintree Steck-Vaughn, 1990.

Baker, Lucy. *Life in the Oceans.* New York: Scholastic, Inc., 1993.

Bramwell, Martyn, *The Oceans.* New York: Franklin Watts, 1994.

Brooks, Felicity. *Seas and Oceans.* Understanding Geography. Tulsa: EDC, 1994.

Ganeri, Anita, *The Oceans Atlas.* New York: Dorling Kindersley, 1994.

Lambert, David. *Seas and Oceans.* New View. Milwaukee: Raintree Steck-Vaughn, 1994.

Talen, Maria. *Ocean Pollution.* Overview. San Diego: Lucent Books, 1994.

FOR OLDER READERS:

Middleton, Nick. *Atlas of the Natural World.* World Contemporary Issues. New York: Facts on File, 1991.

CD Roms:

Geopedia: The Multimedia Geography CD-Rom. Chicago: Encyclopedia Britannica.

Useful addresses:

For more information about the North Sea and the Baltic, write to:

Center for Environmental Education, Center for Marine Conservation, 1725 De Sales Street NW, Suite 500, Washington, DC 20036

Greenpeace International Supporter Services, 176 Kaisersgracht, 1016 DW Amsterdam, The Netherlands

Earthwatch Headquarters, 680 Mount Auburn Street, P.O. Box 403, Watertown, MA 02272-9104

Index